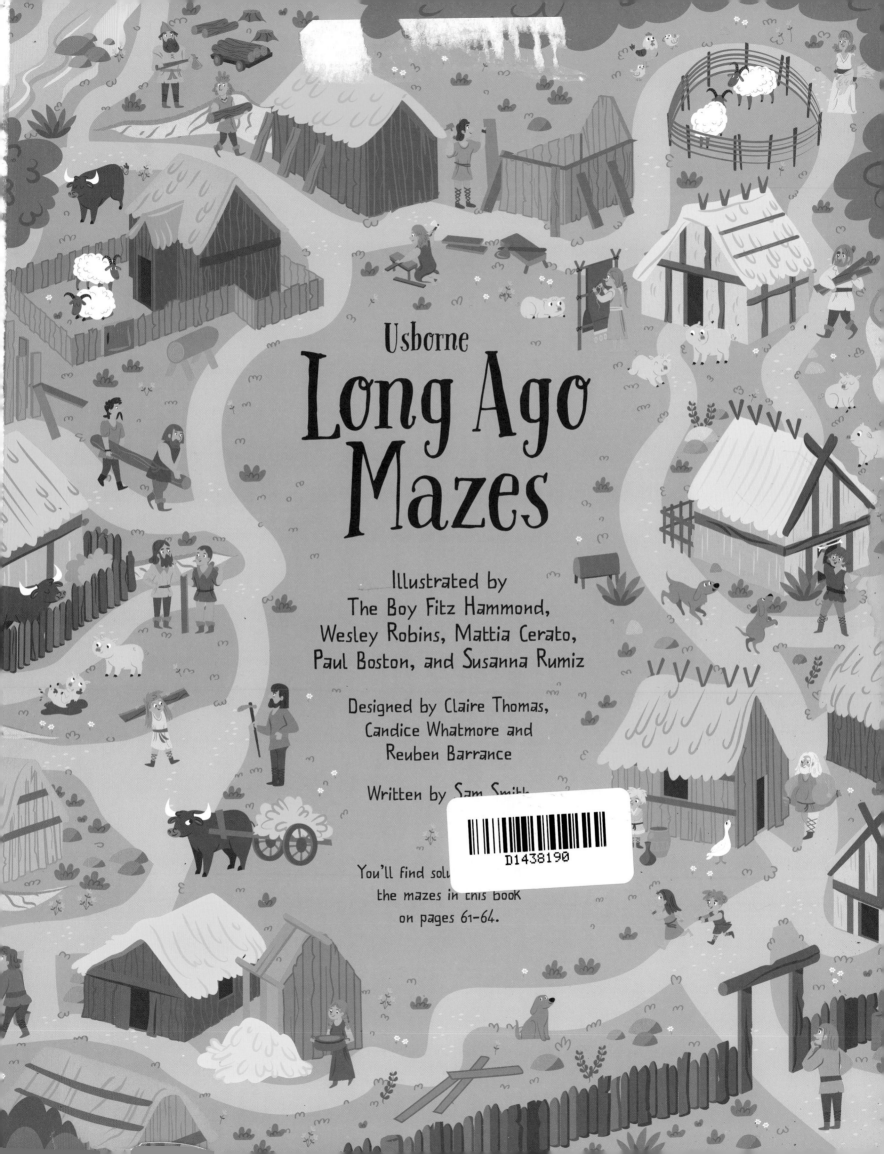

Usborne
Long Ago Mazes

Illustrated by
The Boy Fitz Hammond,
Wesley Robins, Mattia Cerato,
Paul Boston, and Susanna Rumiz

Designed by Claire Thomas,
Candice Whatmore and
Reuben Barrance

Written by Sam Smith

You'll find solutions to
the mazes in this book
on pages 61-64.

Prehistoric predator

A hungry T. Rex is prowling his territory, hunting for food. Can you help the big Alamosaurus round up all the youngsters and rejoin the herd, without taking any path twice?

The herd

Big Alamosaurus

Life on the move

Prehistoric people wandered the land in search of food, never staying in one place for long. Guide Grug along the paths to the cave he's going to shelter in tonight, using the log to cross the river.

Cave

Grug

First farmers

In the Stone Age, people began to plant crops and keep animals. This meant they could live in one place, rather than roaming around. Help Crik harvest all of the barley and return to the village, without retracing his steps.

The village

This is barley.

Crik

Path to the pyramid

Hundreds of Ancient Egyptians are busy building this huge pyramid for Pharaoh Menkaure. Help the water carriers take another jar to the rest area, avoiding any paths blocked by other workers or snakes.

FINISH

Water carriers

5

Early explorers

Long ago, some Polynesian peoples sailed thousands of miles across the sea in canoes, and settled on islands in the Pacific Ocean. Help these settlers steer their canoe to the shore, keeping to the clear water between the waves.

FINISH

START

The Trojan Horse

Greek myth says that a cunning king ended a long siege of Troy by building a huge, hollow horse and hiding soldiers inside. In this scene, the people of the city have unwisely wheeled the horse within their walls. Help the soldiers sneak through the streets, avoiding the guards, so they can open the gates for the rest of the army.

Soldiers

The Oracle at Delphi

In Ancient Greece, people often journeyed to Delphi to seek the advice of its oracle, a high priestess who they believed could foresee the future. Lead Leander up the mountain paths to Delphi, so he can visit the oracle in the Temple of Apollo.

Temple of Apollo

Leander

Elephants in the Alps

Hannibal Barca was a great commander from Carthage, in Africa, who crossed the Alps with elephants in his army to attack Rome. Some of his soldiers have fallen behind in the cold conditions – find a clear path for them, avoiding any snowdrifts, so they can catch up.

START

FINISH

Wonders of the World

In ancient times, there were seven famous "Wonders of the World" that tourists of the age flocked to see. Can you plan a route along the dotted white paths, so Sargon can see all seven wonders on his journey to Jerusalem, without going anywhere twice?

Macedonia

Thrace

Statue of Zeus

Temple of Artemis

Mausoleum at Halicarnassus

Crete

Colossus of Rhodes

Cyprus

Lighthouse of Alexandria

Egypt

Great Pyramid of Giza

Sargon

Cappadocia

Hanging Gardens
of Babylon

Syria

Mesopotamia

Jerusalem

11

Arabia

The Seven Wonders of the Ancient World

Lighthouse of Alexandria
Also called the Pharos, this lighthouse was around 100m tall. It was destroyed by earthquakes.

Great Pyramid of Giza
Built to house the tomb of Pharaoh Khufu, this 147m wonder still stands today.

Colossus of Rhodes
This 33m statue was of the Greek sun-god Helios. It collapsed in an earthquake in 226 BC.

Mausoleum at Halicarnassus
This magnificent tomb was built for Mausolus, a governor in the Persian Empire. It too was destroyed by earthquakes.

Statue of Zeus
This giant seated figure was sculpted at Olympia, Greece. It was destroyed in the 5th century AD.

Hanging Gardens of Babylon
Described as a remarkable series of tiered gardens, the exact site of this wonder is not known.

Temple of Artemis
This Greek temple at Ephesus was rebuilt three times, but only ruins of it remain.

Queen Cleopatra

Cleopatra was the last queen of Ancient Egypt, ruling from her royal palace in Alexandria. Can you find a path through the palace for the visiting Roman general to join Cleopatra on the balcony?

Roman general

Cleopatra

Roman eruption

It's AD 79, and Mount Vesuvius is about to erupt and bury the Roman town of Pompeii beneath a thick blanket of volcanic ash. Find a way for Flavius to warn all these residents and return to the temple steps without doubling back.

Flavius

Gladiator games

Armed men called gladiators were made to fight against each other for public entertainment in Ancient Rome. This show will be starting soon, so guide Gaius to his seat next to Titus without disturbing any of the other spectators. He can only move between rows by using the staircases.

Gaius

Titus

Sigiriya, the Lion Rock

In ancient Sri Lanka, a king called Kashyapa built a grand city and fortress at the site of a huge rock called Sigiriya. Can you lead Kashyapa's men across the landscape to meet the army that has come to attack his new capital?

Kashyapa's men

Attacking army

17

Building in Britain

The Saxons were a European people who settled in Britain in the 5th century. Wilfred has promised to help some of his fellow villagers construct their huts and houses – how can he go to each building site, then head home, without going anywhere twice?

Building sites look like this.

Wilfred's home

19

Wilfred

Viking feast

The Vikings were seafarers from Scandinavia who raided and traded their way along coastlines across Europe. Help Hamar find a way through this feast to put meat on each empty plate, then leave the rest of the joint on the empty plate on Thorolf's table, without having to double back.

Thorolf

Hamar

Legends of the land

Aboriginal peoples in Australia have always told ancient legends about their local landscapes. Can you lead Lang back through the bush in time to hear tonight's tale?

Lang

FINISH

Thieves of the forest

English folklore tells of a heroic outlaw, Robin Hood, who robbed the rich to give to the poor. Can you find Robin a route through Sherwood Forest to his hideout, so he doesn't pass in front of any of the Sheriff of Nottingham's soldiers?

Sheriff's soldier

Robin's hideout

Robin Hood

Mountain meeting

Genghis Khan was a conqueror who founded one of the largest empires in history. Can you guide the visiting monk through the mountain camp, so he can meet and talk with the great leader?

Monk

Genghis Khan

Gifts of gold

Mansa Musa was an emperor of Mali, in Africa, and the richest man who ever lived. Can you help him give gold to all the people in this village as he passes through, without going anywhere twice?

FINISH

Mansa Musa

Joan of Arc's journey

During the Hundred Years' War, a young peasant girl called Joan led French troops to several important victories over the English. Can you guide Joan and her escort to the castle, so she can speak with the king of France?

Medieval mechanics

This Medieval town's clock has stopped striking. Can you help Cuthbert the craftsman reach the tower to repair it, avoiding all the people in the streets in case they delay him?

Cuthbert

The clock tower

29

Aztec travel

Tenochtitlan was the capital of the Aztec Empire, built on a lake island in Mexico. Guide Acalan's canoe along a clear route to the market, then help him find his way on foot to the Greater Temple, using the lowered wooden bridges to cross the canals.

Acalan

Greater Temple

Market

Columbus's course

In 1492, Christopher Columbus set sail from Europe to search for a sea-route to Asia, but instead he found America. Guide Columbus and his crew to the shore and up to the village, so they can trade with the friendly tribesfolk.

Making a masterpiece

Leonardo da Vinci was an Italian artist who painted the world's most famous picture, the Mona Lisa. Find a clear path across the cluttered room so the minstrel can play for Lisa as she poses for the portrait.

Minstrel

FINISH

Amazon exploration

Francisco de Orellana was a Spanish explorer in South America who sailed the length of the Amazon River. Guide his group through the rainforest to ask for food in the native village, using the rocks to cross the fast-flowing water.

Native village

Francisco and crew

Royal ransom

In 1532, Atahualpa, the last Inca Emperor, was captured by Spanish conquerors. To buy his freedom, he told his captors that he would fill an entire room with gold. Lead the three groups of gold-laden llamas along separate routes through the mountains to where Atahualpa is being held.

Atahualpa

35

Majestic monument

The Taj Mahal is a magnificent tomb that was built by Indian emperor Shah Jahan for his wife Mumtaz Mahal. In this scene, the main building has been completed, and the materials are being tidied away. Can you guide Ali the architect to the steps, so he can plan the layout of the gardens?

FINISH

Ali

Banning beards

In 1698, Peter the Great, the ruler of Russia, introduced a tax on beards. None of the bearded men in this picture has paid the tax, so help Pavel the policeman patrol the streets and find each one of them, then return to where he began, without doubling back.

Pavel

Pirate plunder

Many pirates preyed upon ships off the Florida coast in the 1700s. Plot a course so this captain can collect his crew from their island hideouts, then dig up his treasure at the point marked X, without doubling back.

START

FINISH

Boston Tea Party

In 1773, settlers in Boston rebelled against British rule, disguising themselves as Native Americans and hurling hundreds of tea chests into the sea. How can Garth get to his boat and row between the debris to the ship's ladder, so he can take part?

FINISH

Garth's boat

Garth

Precious pottery

An important merchant is visiting this porcelain workshop in China to inspect and buy some of the prized pottery. Which way should he go so he can see each stage of the process without taking the same path twice?

Each stage is marked by a red dot like this.

START

FINISH

43

Royal revelry

Marie Antoinette was a famously fashionable queen of France who threw lavish parties at court. Help the royal servant pick a path through this party to take the cake to the table by the queen.

Royal servant

Marie Antoinette

Kyoto teahouse

Long ago in Japan, teahouses were popular places where people would meet each other and be entertained with music and dancing. Noriko is heading to the Kyoto teahouse – which way should she go to avoid all the puddles?

Kyoto teahouse

Noriko

Crossing a continent

In 1804, two US army officers led an expedition west across America, helped by a Native American woman who translated the languages of local tribes. Can you guide their group along a path across the last stretch of land to the Pacific Ocean?

FINISH

START

Lighting the lamps

Lamplighters walked along the city streets every evening to illuminate London in Victorian times. Help Oliver light all 13 unlit gas lamps in this scene, before heading home. He can walk past lamps that are already lit, but don't take him anywhere twice.

Oliver

Home

Darwin's discoveries

In 1835, the British naturalist Charles Darwin visited the Galápagos Islands and discovered many new types of animals. Plan a route around this island so Darwin can study each animal on the list below at one of their locations. He wants to see all of them in that order, then return to where he started, without retracing his steps.

Darwin

1. Tortoises
2. Iguanas
3. Finches
4. Penguins
5. Crabs
6. Sea Lions

48

Wagons to the West

Between the 1830s and 1860s, many Americans used a wagon route called the Oregon Trail to move thousands of miles across the country and settle on farmlands in the West. David is driving his wagon from Independence to Oregon City – can you lead him along a clear route, so he avoids all of the hazards and blockages shown in the box on the right?

OREGON TERRITORY

Oregon City

CALIFORNIA

UTAH TERRITORY

Hazards and blockages to avoid

Buffalo stampede

Disease area

Flooded road

Wagon congestion

MINNESOTA TERRITORY

WISCONSIN

IOWA

NEBRASKA TERRITORY

KANSAS TERRITORY

Independence

MISSOURI

David

Wartime wounded

Florence Nightingale was a nurse who improved hospital conditions and saved countless lives in the Crimean War. Find her a way around the ward so she can fill every empty glass and finish at the nurses' station without doubling back.

This is an empty glass.

Florence Nightingale

Nurses' station

Looking for Livingstone

In 1871, journalist Henry Morton Stanley set out for Africa to find a missing explorer called David Livingstone. Lead Stanley through the last stretch of jungle to the lakeside village, so he can say the famous words, "Dr. Livingstone, I presume?"

Henry Morton Stanley

Wanted in the Wild West

Life in America's Wild West was dangerous, and people depended upon tough lawmen to protect them. Use the wanted posters to help this town's sheriff find and arrest all five outlaws, in that order, then take them to jail without going anywhere twice.

FREIGHT DEPOT

EST. 1869

RAILROA

LONGHORN STAR

TUMBLEWEED TOWN

BATH HOUSE

WELCOME

GENERAL STORE

STAGE STOP

MAIL OFFICE

1875

J.JACKSON UNDERTAKER

WYATT & SONS BLACKSMITH

Sheriff

WANTED

1. COWARDLY CLIFF

2. THE TEXAS TWINS

3. TERRIBLE TILLY

4. NASTY NATE

Pedal through the park

This Victorian park is packed with children playing and people relaxing in the nice weather. Can you find a way for Fred to pedal his penny-farthing bicycle along the paths to his friends on the other side of the park?

Fred

Fred's friends

Connecting calls

In the early days of telephones, people had to ring an operator before they could speak to someone, so that their call could be connected to the correct line. Follow Dr. Lennon's call along the line, then help Emma Nutt, the first female operator, pick the right line to put it through to Mr. Robertson.

Miss Emma Nutt
Switchboard Operator

A B C D E

Mrs. P. Wilbur

Mr. A. Smith

Mr. J. Robertson

Dr. S. Lennon

Miss B. Merry

South Pole snow

From 1910 to 1912, Captain Robert Scott led a British expedition trying to reach the South Pole. Can you guide his team along smooth snow to the hut, so they can make their final preparations?

Scott and team

Jazz Age journey

During the 1920s, jazz music took cities like New Orleans and New York by storm, and inspired young people across America. Find where Suzie is supposed to sing tonight, then steer her car along clear roads to the club.

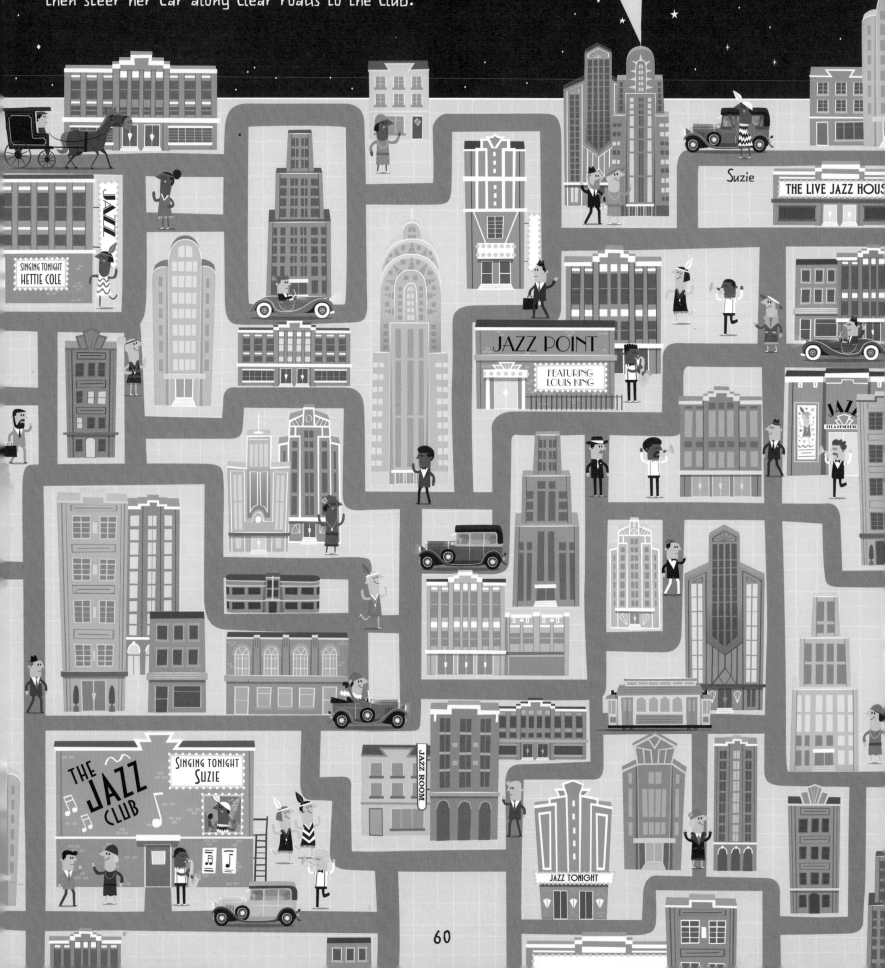

2. Prehistoric predator

3. Life on the move

4. First farmers

5. Path to the pyramid

6. Early explorers

7. The Trojan Horse

8. The Oracle at Delphi

9. Elephants in the Alps

10-11. Wonders of the World

12. Queen Cleopatra

13. Roman eruption

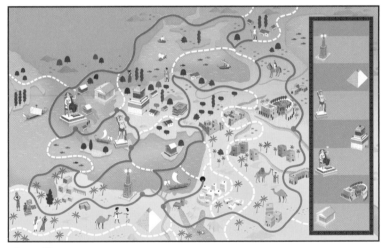

14-15. Gladiator games

16-17. Sigiriya, the Lion Rock

SOLUTIONS

18-19. Building in Britain

20-21. Viking feast

22. Legends of the land

23. Thieves of the forest

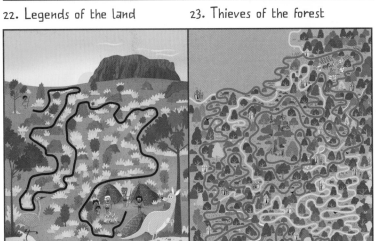

24-25. Mountain meeting

26. Gifts of gold

27. Joan of Arc's journey

28-29. Medieval mechanics

30. Aztec travel

31. Columbus's course

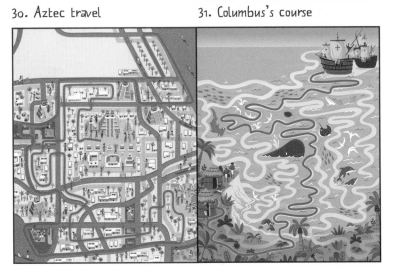

32. Making a masterpiece

33. Amazon exploration

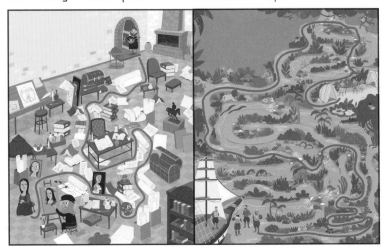

34-35. Royal ransom

36-37. Majestic monument

38-39. Banning beards

40. Pirate plunder   41. Boston Tea Party

42-43. Precious pottery

44. Royal revelry   45. Kyoto teahouse

46. Crossing a continent   47. Lighting the lamps

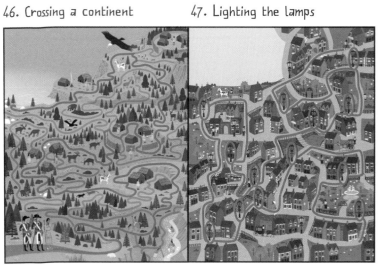

48-49. Darwin's discoveries

50-51. Wagons to the West

52. Wartime wounded   53. Looking for Livingstone

54-55. Wanted in the Wild West

56-57. Pedal through the park

58. Connecting calls   59. South Pole snow

60. Jazz Age journey

Acknowledgements

Edited by Sam Taplin

First published in 2019 by Usborne Publishing Ltd. 83–85 Saffron Hill, London ECIN 8RT, England. www.usborne.com